Strange
Valentine

Crab Orchard Series in Poetry
FIRST BOOK AWARD

Massac Creek #9, 2004, by John Folsom

Strange Valentine

Crab Orchard Review

&

Southern Illinois University Press

CARBONDALE

A. Loudermilk

Printed in the United States of America

08 07 06 05   4 3 2 1

Frontispiece: Massac Creek #9, 2004, a photograph by John Folsom.
Courtesy of Newzones Gallery of Contemporary Art, Calgary, Canada.

The Crab Orchard Series in Poetry is a joint publishing venture of Southern Illinois
University Press and *Crab Orchard Review.* This series has been made possible by the
generous support of the Office of the President of Southern Illinois University and the
Office of the Vice Chancellor for Academic Affairs and Provost at Southern Illinois
University Carbondale.

Crab Orchard Series in Poetry Editor: *Jon Tribble*
First Book Award Judge for 2004: *Julia Kasdorf*

Library of Congress Cataloging-in-Publication Data
Loudermilk, A.
Strange Valentine / A. Loudermilk.
  p. cm. — (Crab Orchard series in poetry)
  I. Title. II. Series: Crab Orchard award series in poetry.
PS3612.O785S77 2005
811'.6—dc22
ISBN 0-8093-2661-2   2005002512

Printed on recycled paper. ♻

The paper used in this publication meets the minimum requirements of American
National Standard for Information Sciences—Permanence of Paper for Printed
Library Materials, ANSI Z39.48-1992. ∞

For Hollie and Afton

Nothing human disgusts me unless it's unkind, violent.

— Hannah in *THE NIGHT OF THE IGUANA*
by Tennessee Williams

Contents

THE POCKETBOOK WOMEN

THE LAST CALL

TEETH IN THE GARDEN & OTHER EVIDENCE

Acknowledgments

Grateful acknowledgment to the following publications in which poems in this collection previously appeared:

- *Cider Press Review*—"For the Great-Aunt Who Collected Clocks"
- *The Gay and Lesbian Review*—"The Undescending Man"
- *The James White Review*—"After the Accident: The Evenings & the Nights of Cole Porter" and "Belt"
- *The Louisville Review*—"For the Great-Aunt Who Never Married"
- *The Madison Review*—"Trash w/ Dog," "The Radium Dial," and "Mema's Hat"
- *Margie*—"Not Even Doublewide" and "Married Women: A Sideshow"
- *The Mississippi Review*—"For the Great-Aunt Who Married Twice"
- *Porcupine*—"She Hardly Ever Says a Word"
- *Rhino 2000*—"The Pocketbook Women of You-Be-Dam Holler"
- *Southern Poetry Review*—"Proof"
- *Sow's Ear*—"First National Bank, *a fantasy*"
- *Tin House*—"Buckshot" and "The Smallest Woman in the World Who Once Posed on the Lap of the Richest Man in America Considers the Bad Dreams of the Tallest Man Who Ever Lived"
- *Unlikely Stories*—"Crooked County (At The Bluebird with You)" and "El Diablo Nuevo"
- *The Yalobusha Review*—"Mema's Funeral"

Several poems in this collection appeared in the chapbook *The Daughterliest Son* (Swan Scythe Press, 2002).

"The Pocketbook Women of You-Be-Dam Holler" appeared in *New Voices: University and College Poetry Prizes 1989–1998.*

DARING LOVE

Daring Love

I am daring love to be anything else,
to be on its best behavior wicked, to be heartache
in its prime. Love, nod yes, the noggin
of a great disease. Make chain gangs by design,
love; be phantom brawling the nursery, be darkness.

Love, a cooing shadow when a stranger
takes me into his car. Love is my spiced breath,
love cuts teeth. Love unwinds iambic vines
down unrhymed alleyways, jeweled yet innocent weeds
casually blooming the balled tongues of children.
Love dedicates itself, all ruby-sucked thumbs,
to the stewing cradle at the foot of a stranger's
gut. Tell me truth, love: why want his mouth
that toils like a bad taste after the mint
of the moon?

Just leave husk and gristle. I dare you—

be the reason my mother hated to be touched.
Thirty years with a man who refused homecomings
and proms, married without mentioning love. My mother.
Every night she bleached the coaldust out of his clothes,
tasted in his mouth the coalmine, the scuttle, the coal.
You are that smoked winter, love, admit it. You waltzed
his black lung, her wallflower cancer. The ICU nurse
said my mother loved me. Love, are you an empty stare
as the heart, your celebrated domain,
latches its last door?

I am daring love to be anything else,
to be heathen in a red room, to be God's love
for Job, to be kicked dog. Grind your spotlight
on the daughterliest sons. Leave a little despair,
love, be what the least of us can claim.

Inheritance

My mother's duty, some polecat heirloom—
to never quite lounge, goldleaf bruises
upside her cheek. So lovely, so lovely

no one dared to look. My mother is gone
and all over my father's house I drape apology,
bathe face-down deep in gunpowdered roses,

rich with meat grease. Getting it, getting it
done. Strictly his son. The secret: cold quiet,
a flotsam stock on the stove. Mother is gone

and all over my father's house I hide her jewelry,
her words unbroken. On the last day of her life
she died. Left me. A verb inside a noun, the will

to matter without speaking.

Belt

(If you're not 18 please hang up now)

Late night in the unease
of a Missouri trailer park where no one
is native, in the common darkness of the displaced,

I sit on the kitchen floor, whispering to him. My robe open

in the delicate light of an open refrigerator.
My stepmother asleep on the living room couch. I listen
to the man on the telephone say I am nothing
between my legs but a woman
and a poor excuse. I say nothing
violently, and at his order say   "Thank you,

yes." (I remember my father's shoulders,
the broad ironed bed of his back, spiders
under his arms. He showed me what
setting the table meant, giggling bent
over the basin, singing soprano.) Every father

has a belt, the man tells me, for boys
who should have been girls.

"17," I tell the truth.
"No, I've never done that," I lie.

Thank you. Yes.

Stepmother

I landed in red. Red
gaudily breaks apart, red
mother carpet rolls down
her reddest corridor. Red
blessed red, grant me beginning
in her tongue-tied flames so red,
in her trailer park, in her sad made bed.
Hanging laundry she spits,

Mexicans get nastier than kids—
Don't ever lend them cigarettes.

I landed in red. Red
is the angry woman who bites her tongue
and feeds her children like a bird.

Not Even Doublewide

Light comes on. Smoke breaks out.
They—in nightclothes, in fits—
open the blue trailer door, fall
to the dew and scream at my fire.

They think I am still asleep
inside the burning blue trailer.

There are houses with so much
banister and window and hearth.
Houses never stopped at red lights.
Houses without the hazards on.

We had little.
Little burns quick.

Rent

My bed is on the landlord's floor. His men are in the basement
clattering up dirt rooms where old wood smokes sunlight
chronometrically. They address the rotting timbers. The men
are in the basement, the teeth are on the saw, small mice
they worry, worry, & bed is the breadth of my landlord's floor.

I love him so much I haven't touched myself for three days.

First floor, my bed is on the floor. Sing mattress springs
to the trio of hammers against you & I will think of Matthew
in a v-neck romantically. Our bodies full of drum. The men
are in the basement, a claw is at bent nails, my morning
knocks *hurry, hurry*—rent is due on the landlord's floor.

First National Bank, *a fantasy*

I am the teller, window five, hello
and welcome home. The stars are out tonight.
No copper constellations these, no sir.

A rattling storm of silver dollars breaks.
All pockets begging wide as empty birds.

Just so his hands are watermarked. When held
against the light I see   Andromeda.
The counterfeiter loves with perfect change.

Spanking Birds

I don't believe you when you

■

The empty flower pots outside are full of snow.

■

want me, reach for me. I hear you
knocking shave
& a haircut. In my apartment, jiggling
the handle. Petting my fires. Birds caged here
like spankings. Instead
you take a slotted spoon to an empty kettle & stir the kitchen
into a bell. You know the mother sauces.

■

I don't believe you, my body always untouched in service
& shadow, removed from the reaches of

■

Begonias got blooming down. Cold,
peaked, they bloom fragile—a papercut. They bloom
no matter & you never really know what's hit.

■

Hot, Mild, or Fire? You work the drive-thru
embezzling pocket change, the grease of 40 hours
on your skin, in my sheets. You are bored
with spoons & *not yet.* You take off your shirt
each night, knowing
I just want you near—your hands
hot conspirators, your mouth
my secret place, where I fly from the reaches of

■

men who never kiss.

El Diablo Nuevo

Destitute in vintage suit, all pinstripes
point downtown. When we're out of cigarettes

he walks like a rifle, trigger
unstifled, to the full-blooded Amoco—
his pockets all sold-out of skunk

weed and micro-plaid acid. Among his fine
features, no counterfeits: hand lost at cheek,
all straight
teeth, he is a most beautiful drug addict.

When we're caught in the rain,
                        the rain doubles.

Way out of town we wade where my dad's creek forks.
He accepts all
flattery. All day on Saturdays. His every tattoo
lavished with it. Swimmer,

swimmer, take the sweltering
day anonymously under
water, to river, to sea. Dictator of naked, narcosis

of nitrogen. Pisser in the deep end, tread down
the rapture, the whorl of my thumbprint.

Strange Valentine

One tug and it's valentine's day. You turn against me
stone against stone and we unravel all night
into this little fire then that—without sounds like yes
or no. I want to say I'm sorry but I don't. I won't

see you again, not after you've seen me, thrown light onto me

and I can't I just can't do anything but hide
tighter against your body, somewhere
where I could be anybody—kiss your back
your hip under your beard. You've never met me before.

Strange Valentine II

The last thing you did was leave abruptly. Gone

like valentine's day. Yet even it'll return
with or without you, throbbing
and wagging its red finger at the lonely.
Lonely was the first thing you told me.
Winter hitchhiker, dressed for a long walk
home, you've got no number to give me
and I've no way to find you in the woods

where you all alone hold everything I don't know about you.

Agoraphobia

Little man winter in the waxpaper apron, summer needs gagging
quick while the hot plane of its face is still
turned away. Curtains pin themselves here by noon, shadows
solder these rooms. The strongest lamp-bulbs have broken

their filaments. When the macaw on its black cage
stretches its clipped wings, the sound of feathers
startles me; like the whole house

breathing out in a rush, like someone
cracked the door. Closed the door is mother.

Open the door is father.

THE STEEPEST CAKE

Married Women: A Sideshow

500 bolts off-white, my bride. With all
that gas in her belly, she rumbled
like a kicked bee box. Titanic lady,
she left me, too big for her legs,
too buxom to vacuum. So pretty
in the face. I loved her. Everyone
laughed. Hippopotamus. I loved you.

(2 Women: Alice the house all premature
gray & Berl the smoker, horse-dentured
or toothless. Each a punchline. Everyone
knew. The big lady's dead now & Berl she
mows yards in summer, cleans out gutters
May & November. Every spring a poem
for A's birthday from B
w/ love on the last page of the Gazette.)

Barn-woman, my housewife. With all
those streamlining tricks: she crossed
her arms downward to bully her gut
& feature her wrists, actually so
delicate. Blue-slippered mama,
everyone stared. Your heart said stop
& they cut you open. Polished honey
flowed from my sweetheart. Sugarhips.
Tubaist. Star of my barge & railroad car.

Mema's Hat

Sometimes they vomit with heart,
the nurse on the phone clips her sentence.

Between nausea and an oxygen tank, my mother's
mother continues to smoke. Salem 100's. She always
smoked with perfect posture and lipstick. In an all-white

housing project in Jonesboro, quadrupled and sewn twice up

the middle, on a bedsore that wants bone, she's got three rooms
to sail: recliner, microwave, bed. She watches westerns,
she's quit her story, she tucks her cordless phone

into the apron pocket of her walker, she's due a permanent.
Where went that strut? Heels clicking like accountants.

■

Walking through a crowd I remember myself as a woman

walking through a crowd remembering herself as a boy
parading through the house with Mema's hat

on crooked. I've got the kind of name that tiptoes.
I've got elders to respect. I've got a stroke under my bed
reminiscing the left side of her smile. I've got other things

to do. My mother would rather be home watching the satellite.

■

One more time, the nurse tells us, *and her body*
won't take it, As if her body could go on strike

from her opinion. Spitfire unto backfire, her name is the kind

that chases other names around with a hoe. Her name starts
with a secret L. Her name changed seven times in three states.

Midday weather drenches the Missouri bootheel, floods

the tri-state, and she speaks of 1937 and all that water
coming right up the steps, up the steps of the post office
where the boys gathered. And my mother's father, *he'd be*

sitting there where there wasn't anywhere else to go

and I would just go wild inside. She presses her fist
to her chest. Mema that loved hard. Mema that drank
40 years, lit up half the twentieth century.

Kicked Dog

Kicked dog, I know your grief,
why you don't bother to tell the moon
your troubles. It belongs to the night,
deaf and godless, it won't hear you.
It is cold and breathless. Its heart
is chalk, it has no time for lyrics.

      Where's your man gone, kicked dog?
      Left the house without a word?

Dog I know your need, why you stay
at his feet like a stone face-down. Someday
when everyone has left him, you'll be there,
him ripening on the stair. For 39 rings
of the telephone, you'll taste love,
hold it in your mouth.

      Where's your man gone, kicked dog?
      North, south, east, west.

Talk Like a Sailor

We never love each other with our mouths
open & only when it's flat drunk dark do we fuck
facing—when I kneel at his mouth, the confessional,
& whisper to the little red priest inside,

I've lied, I told my lover I despised him.
(Honesty: a neckline he only buys plunging,
his bitten kiss there chromatic, blooming.)
My criminal has a handsome face, dark eyes

like hours of suspicion, moments of trust. I look
prim next to my criminal, our joke on this subdivided
district so 2nd Baptist. Talk like a sailor, says he.
Cuss a blue streak. He adores my indelicacy

at night, when it grifts him to sleep. Under
his right jaw: today's shaving scar. I know
should I endear his flaws, he'd never forgive
mine. Night idles on its axle & I play him

by the goatee, spit toothsome songs about stars
falling & petty cash, room keys & ice
buckets, zirconias & hostages & that time
we took pictures & this heart my risked

fortress, my throttled valentine. Like a sailor,
he says. *I'll give lousy eulogy.* Cuss a blue
streak. *Hatred is loving too hard.* When he wakes,
I call him a bastard, make the bed with old fire.

The Steepest Cake

I made the wedding cake steep
when I sunk

my busiest hand, an animal cross with nature,
into virgin batter.
My creature fist
in that cake—groom couldn't know as he fed bride,
two months pregnant,
that it punched down
her throat a taste of despair. Ceremony—
she'll never know
the ceremony of a dare,
what we waged as children in the chickenhouse.
She'll never answer
to the anniversary
of a secret. She tears down the bedclothes, prays
you into amen
and out again Matthew
Mark Luke&John BookoftheActs Romans. Your daughters,

breech births hungry
and loud about it.

She Hardly Ever Says a Word

Weakness has no lilt, really. No fainting
spells. No housebroken eclipse. No wild sighs
into handkerchiefs. A baby sprawled open
all plush & nap-fattened: his strength
comes through like teeth. *Quietly.* These rooms
are asleep, the pipes not speaking, water
rests in their elbows. *Silently.* (She pins up
her hair—fanatical crown of pentecostal
cursive—& wields her unsung tongue
over underbite: 30 crooked birds
perched in a shut place. They sing only
of things too fragile to hold in your pocket.)

While the Pentecostal Men Are in Their Cars,
a fantasy

The women beat light by half
an hour. Twenty four
waders in the river at dawn,

they

wash away the clothes
of miscarried daughters, fathom
the mud again & shores
according to water. The women

unpin

their hair & the water stops
rolling. They pin up again their hair
& the river, pinned up, goes to church.

Spinster

Her voice needles me knowing
where my voice sleeps
soundest. Her mother's lick,
a silent fit, clean. I am so out of love
I can't tell when the morning 7 breaks
the berry from its twig, the hour
when straw catches from a first cigarette
the fire of going at it one more time. So whirs

her fan: night
into day, hot
into heat, sky

carrying moon such a way
that an old woman

—without a husband, without a wife—

       predicts a boy.

Mema's Funeral

Blaring sun:
summer's opinion.

She was not a summer baby and fire was not her element,

astrologically,
believe it or not.

Born in November she was water, buried on the longest day in July,

next to the husband
she never got over.

Her sister points out where the house used to be, the store, this road they
hitched

into town
on Saturdays

for boys when they were sixteen. And now, a procession makes the town's traffic.

The cemetery
overgrown with men.

Shitbanger Girl

She's cool. She takes her cigarette breaks with us
even though she don't smoke.

Her dad used to call that car *baby*.

Now she drives the hell out of it. Says she'll drive it into the ground.
She'll take the longest way every time. Over gravel and hauling dope
or whatever. The supervisors here don't like her but they can't catch her
at nothing. She's got her degree in something—she knows things. She
takes breaks with us, tells us how people walk each other like dogs.

She calls me Uptown Girl. I used to be more stylish.

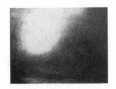

THE WORKING BODY

The Undescending Man

The man in my mouth who sings falsetto
has nothing to do with the woman who flashes a blur
of peter & kootch behind a tolled curtain. Dive with me

into fountains, surface twice as wet as wet. I don't know
how to love myself out of such waters. On stage I fold
myself down the middle: for ladies for gents for

the sake of show: my girl leg shaved, spitcurl
opposed to sideburn. I am all I need on a desert island,
the ticket grinder sells me. I'll trade a kiss & my vote

for a little tender catcall & your boots off. The price
to see behind the trap door in my costume is the answer
to this question: Who about me do you hate the most?

Or—with the lights off—who might you love?

Threading Needles, *a fantasy*

Without hands, arms, legs—buttons

mind your needle like thread
minds the needle's eye. With teeth

& the little god gave you, you

sew porchlight into the shadow
of your suitcase, glancing along
the bias of the crowd. Your mother

waits in the wings, scissors
ready. You don't miss

what you never had. From hay

you spin a Sunday dress, lace
you cut from milk; sleeve
by sleeve you hold the world

like your mother holds you. Then you

stitch that cryptic grin: spotlights purr.
Unless filled with communion wine,

what good is a thimble to you?

You hem the stage curtain & every
ring-finger in the audience gets pricked.

The Radium Dial

1983:

How to tell hot spots in winter? The snow's
lost to mud, yokel dogs tumored. He's no liar,
the only geiger counter in town—always on duty

in Death City, Illinois. 125 counts per minute,
250 counts: the beery woods
behind the high school a hot spot, landfills
hum a sick steam,
route 6 trailers court their radioactive outskirts,

and the Dial—dismantled by the government
(brickdust by boiler into
armed portions) and buried all around town—
still in its own absence ticks

beneath the lot where it stood
40odd years at 500 counts per minute.

1983 ON 1932:

"If you've got money, you've got it
licked, the whole world."

"This is a picture of the girls that all
worked at the Radium Dial. They all worked
with my sister. And that was the time
of the Depression. And all the girls worked
with her and they just like my sister all
painted the faces of the clock."

"Peg's trouble started when she had a tooth pulled."

1932:

Littler
like the clock's, her hands daintied time itself

with the all-American convenience of glowing
in the dark. It took radium
and a skeptical brush to spook the clock's expression,

to give 3 a.m. the whisper of 3 a.m. without a light on.
Radium Dial girls by the hundreds were 16
and tricounty, 18 in fur collars, 19 and 20
on the town. (They didn't know
how radium hides like a doubt
in our bones.) They were 21
and newlywed, 22 and late again. Dial-painters,

attending to one numeral at a time
around the clock. Sometimes 1's first; five 1's,
two 2's, then 0 and the commoners. Southpaws
might start at 5's paunch. The odds have angles, there
are hips on an 8. 9 is hunchback. 4 a doomed house. 11,
twins. 12, disciples. With every second hand iota,
every speck of afternoon, girls twirled
the brushes in their mouths as trained—
for a finer   *point.*

And the superstitious began with 7.

WWII:

In bedrooms everywhere radium hands accuse

radium minute rings of losing midnight
to that other 12.
                    A two-faced little
wall-clock aperch the theater's EXIT
tells the wrong time to abandoned credits.
                    Ouija boards

gleam yes in cellar, no in closet, goodbye.

Even grandfather
                is radium-handed. As is

the oven timer. The barometer. The north star's
gauges ripen at dusk on our pilots' dashboards.

The most popular bombs fall branded
with radium crosses. Watches everywhere
                watch back.

1951:

Music played when they x-rayed her. Mrs. Marie Rossiter

tapped a thumb knuckle on her collar bone. Biannually
strung up for atomic research, her body (classified

dial painter) set nuclear exposure standards,

got vaulted for body-burden radioactivity assessment.
"Different record?" the nurse asked, restrapping her
busy arm. "A waltz?" (Her body's secret:
contamination. Her secret body

a hot spot,

porous, to-be-broken. Irredeemable. Lest she forget
her friends died regularly. Lest she forget—the priest,
even he kept his distance: housecalling the eucharist

and splitting.) With a jug of pee and
a tarot of x-rays, how could she not know
that soon enough something like a car accident
would tear her down at the hemline.

1958:

On television: Under the sofa—

in their Sands Hotel room—Lucy
stashes her geiger counter.

Ricky has forbidden her uranium hunting.

Under the sofa, Lucy's geiger counter clicks
in fits over guest star Fred MacMurray's wristwatch

when he bends down to tie his shoe. Radium gag

begets car chase.

WWII:

Radium imported for clocks reprocessed
into polonium blasts a light only a blind girl
on the other side of the world could fathom.

1932:

The factory geared-up palpitated
gossipless. Too busy

to talk. Every room a hundred girls
making money,
turning out alarms, illuminating the ons
and offs. Marie's trio, wasting

their break, scraped
shine from the morning jars, painted each other starry

in a broom closet: one glowering,

another stippled
burlesque. Mutton-chopped. Cyclopsed. Ritzy. A mutiny
minor in a factory groped to the boiler with so much

shine . . . its smirk so pretty
in the dark, its blizzard's tail, its brillig foot
clawed like a tub's, its cricket noise everywhere.

Thalidomide

She never did sleep well. Little pill

helped her sleep. I kicked a lot. I

kept her awake at night. She never

did sleep well. Little pill hushed us.

House by house, pill by pill: utopias

never do sleep well, war-worried

& tin-foiled. I nagged her heartbeats,

becoming something unbecoming. Yes

& no. Not exactly. Not quite. Like those

thousands unlike anyone else who

turned into your children anyway.

The Smallest Woman in the World Who Once Posed on the Lap of the Richest Man in America Considers the Bad Dreams of the Tallest Man Who Ever Lived

His mother even on tiptoe   no longer can she straighten his tie.
Even when he was a boy   his father inherited his shirts.

Pituitary giant, pathologically tall. Apologetic—

his height is not his fault he claims. At 22 he'll die
still growing. Foot trouble in Alton, Illinois. Across yoked beds,
his room crowded with him, he dreams perhaps
of Babylon
& Pisa. Gravity,
the master, hums as he collapses.

■

And the anatomists wait   behind far-flung drapes.
Undertakers stand on chairs   measuring the horizon

for his wake-wear. Major Atom & Admiral Dot

battle over the territory between his lifeline
& thumbnail. Jack schemes. Chandeliers tangle
like flocks of stars charging his hat from all sides
at once. Sling shot
stones with Old Testament intentions graze
his periphery,
but it's wartime
when only bombers could tease his reach.

■

Every cubit & span of him   measured. Altitude
& inseam. Shoe size makes   headlines. Weighs

21 stones. At 7:

"The Tallest Boy Scout." Mr. Robert Wadlow—
hardly a sideshow in his suit & tie. His chair built-to-scale
rocks stage center all the way to St. Louis. He takes

a million 10¢ questions about
the weather up there, his fear of falling down, how he fits
into voting booths, his watch
band & leg
braces, dropsy, how he climbs narrow stairs.

∎

We live & will die   on opposite sides of the pituitary, opposite
sides of the Atlantic.   From the lap of America, little me

misses my mother in Germany. His mother tiptoes

over winter, the broken sidewalk, in his dream
of the backyard. Ice worries him. His leg-brace
scrapes his leg infectious. We are not so miraculous
after all. He is no taller than my last breath
which shall rise
as my body hides
in a room crowded with gas.

After the Accident:
The Evenings & the Nights of Cole Porter

EVENINGS.

Across the shoulders of a young valet,
his legs dangle,
shoes new. Society friends pace the hall
in black-tie, in pearls—Truman,
Kitty Carlisle—convened at this iron lung

of a suite only to wait for their host
to be carried, propped like a Queen Anne chair
at the dining room table. He doesn't speak,

he listens. Gossip from green rooms,
anecdotal scandal, easy
actors. Opening nights. Who Truman hates. And then bolting,
crashing, memory kicks at a silence: so the riding horse rolls
over & over on poor Cole Porter.

NIGHTS.

He crawls with the grain of the floor
to get to the naked actor across the room
who says, *Do you want this? Come get it.*

Under the arch of two potent legs, he is broken,
his eyes revolving up to the man he knows
will step away, baiting him with a nightly song:
Drag yourself like a bridal train —

And he does, around the study
for half a cruel hour
until the man gives in. Cole Porter
pulls himself up a body like this,
thigh by shoulder by height.

Ugly Dares the Marriage Vow

The Ugliest Woman in the World
sings a love song in three languages. Her audience

whispers, looks

her up & down, frills over bald palms. How in the world
to love its ugliest? Her exhibitor, he proposes. Their vows
tremble in print until the boy is born: swaddled in hair
& asphyxiated. She dies a mother & the sight of her—
her exhibitor, he deodorizes: their baby in a sailor suit

gets fixed to a bar like a parrot, obliviously a kiss away.

■

Some little flower, a curtsy-petaled delicacy—

part of the act, perhaps: sweet nothing
for a bearded lady. On the balls of her feet,
avoiding gazes by the cluster, she crosses
birth into death & finds herself on the same stage

shedding fame,
daring her widower to look away, to turn out the light.

THE POCKETBOOK WOMEN

No One's Favorite Aunt Died Blonde

This is not a true story
but names have been changed
to protect the never-so-innocent,
the high strung yet house-trained,

the big mouth. She's blonde for good.

In aluminum, blue with satin
interior, demure but shop-soiled—buttoned
up in the wool she wore to weddings, tacky
with toothpaste droppings—she looks
like hell boxed up
to go. Her nieces pair words: folding

& chair. A game from: vacations &

psychoanalysis. Jo says thunder, Maggie
answers lightning. Deer & tick. Canker
& sty. Hanker & chief. Cheap

& casket. Good. Bye. Never again
to sigh over Sinatra. Never again

will her roots show.

For the Great-Aunt Who Collected Clocks

When they all strike at once I'll be dead
she said
every time her clocks staggered the new hour

When they strike all in a row it's crib death
little breaths
purling one last three a.m. in the nursery

When all they strike is midnight midnight
palindromic
cuckoos excoriate their minute hands

When striking cabal they all stand alone
mentholated baritones
tall in dark corners & each a husband

The Great-Aunt Who Collected Clocks Meets the Burglar

She's forgot to turn the clocks back an hour & when
they ring they'll ring four when it's three & she gets
up at six so tonight swigs an extra breath every second,

every second she stares at midnight, digital in its scandal

with the moon skyridden. How they conspire against her tides
into sleep, into sleep, into sleep: into nightmaring the cellar
door unlocked & silverware drawers wrenched across a red kitchen

linoleum, premiering the butcher knife in a black man's hands.

She's forgot to set the clocks back an hour & when
she goes to church in the morning only she will have lived
this hour no one lives, this hour between one second & the next

disowned with every clock she winds minus for daylight

savings. Blindly, she makes port of every room keeping time.
Upstairs, the alarms: her room & the guest room where sisters
now sleep, where her eldest son wept curse words & stashed

whiskey before his father died. After. Still

there are these nights (she swears) when shots ring out
in a deuce of bells, when the burglar breaks a window
& the getaway night revs, when the ambulance never arrives

in time, when the clocks and all their arabics & romans

grieve not. Downstairs, the grandfathers: in dimestore nightlight
she opens them like robed men. Takes the hour. She hears breathing
& footsteps in the kitchen. She hears breathing & footsteps

in the kitchen. Catches her son taking twenty from her purse again.

For the Great-Aunt Who Attempted Suicide

Slick magnolia drape over the kitchen window,
tea boiling, & the screen door locked to shut
her out. Uncle Vandell upstairs not talking

to her, playing the widower again. The kitchen
is tideless. Daughters & nieces despise him—
all barber strop & onion birthstone & clank

of knife & fork on a finished plate. Blinds
pinch the picture window, TV lamp
off, even the nightlatch used against her.

Uncle Vandell upstairs not talking to her,
tea boiling away again. Neighbors never
suspect her tethered walks around the house.

Peculiar tonight her leaving the yard. The evening
sun cribs itself, sky trellises its stars. She
considers driftwood & all currented things, how

the dirty river racks its thoughtless prizes.

She Talks a Mile a Minute

Soap stars mingle twelve steps at a time, toasting her
with sparkling cider,
paparazzi in constellation. My great-aunt
offers the reporter a cheese on cheese cracker sandwich.
He refuses. I take two. She does not turn down the television.

We are not alone, she quotes her husband. *The miraculous
all around us: duckbill platypus, Loch Ness, abominables.*

                ▪

My grandfather's brother is 76 and lost in the Pacific Northwest
searching the boggy creeks for tracks to plaster-cast, for a myth
to videotape, for a dark man or a man in the dark or the dark itself

as it dwells in the vanishing woods

sweating through its hairy suit. My aunt has given twelve interviews
since she rang the police to tell them neither her husband
nor his Sasquatch have returned from what she titles *Ed's Safari.*

Today is her fifth day as front page competition

for the Mississippi, flooding
into August. She's rouged to impress *The Gazette.*

                ▪

For the great-aunt who kidnaps any spotlight.
Who matches any camera's dime-splitting flash

with a loot of hip and dimple. Who pranks
neighbors and religious channel prayer warriors
and my mom. Who on a dare

called *Lucy* at Klondike 5. Who dared me
to call *Barney Miller* and ask for Fish.

Who never dresses down
for *All My Children,* such carbonated galas

as the bomb-threatened dedication
of a hospital's new wing. She hushes us.
She's got to see this. Some Hungarian ex-husband
declares to Erica Kane: "This isn't how I wanted you to find out

I was still alive."

■

If the sideshow wouldn't come to us
he'd take us to the side. He always had to see it

first, show me second. We'd gawk—

hold hands. He'd ask to kiss me
in the shadow of a hermaphrodite

and others propped upright, barked about.
All those primates. I hope he brings me back a souvenir,

a horrible toe.

For the Great-Aunt Who Never Married

A lettuce leaf in soup will take up the grease.
If hiccups, drink water through a handkerchief.
Bury a rooster twice as deep as coon dogs dig.
Restring pearls that aren't really pearls so

they at least look like new. Hide his first name,
bottom of the button box. Whisper it to the well
spiders. Never ask God for a single thing. Always
dry white stockings in a dark room. Take the shine

off a black dress. Boil clothespins. Weep. Into
sinkholes. Into a nest of hull & down. Bank the fire
noiselessly in sickrooms. Hush windows with gauze.
Pray for loved ones in alphabetical order. Match

scratches on white walls? Cat pee on suede slippers?
Mother clouding the vinegar? Feather ticking
stinking of a dying old woman? Try bicarbonate
of soda under the arms. A blindfold on her pillow.

Mahogany cake with sleeping powders. Salt the floor.
Slip away to meet him & your mouth goes dry. Creeks
run over—it's spring—& maybe she'll nap her heart
stopped. (To the bright hand of God like a moth

she'll swing.) Hyperacidity? Dirty velour? Foreign body
in eye? Wall mice? To know if the telephone rings
while you're away: carbon paper between clapper & bell.
Open your mouth every other kiss. He'll love you

more. Or he won't love you at all. Never
be jealous of your mother just because she's dying
a widow. Don't hate men that cuss. Don't cuss men.
Restring your pearls again. Turn the mattress. Turn

her bed to face east. Turn the house inside out.

For the Great-Aunt Who Married Twice

It was divorce when I pawned the ring,
she answers today's fiancé. Joppa to Metropolis
across the bridge to Kentucky, married on the way
& honeymooning a new year lease just north
of Southside Motors. With a diamondless needle
on the record player, there's nothing else to do.

The mattress springs in shivaree blather
me in virgin key. Behind blue dot draperies,
Husband 2, I rise for you: be-bop of biscuit
dough. I am blind knocking in black stockings
& bigamy in brand new bikini. & you—brooder
of my brouhaha—blinkered by blankets,
you are my all time favorite.

The bathwater runs all out hot, blaring
steam over their make-do wedding clothes
(flagged across shut windows)
before going out to the restaurant
where paper roses fret over candlelight
& the piano player is colored. They'll roll in
like dice, like there's nowhere else to roll.

The Great-Aunt Who Never Let a Nigger
in Her House Meets the Colored Nurse

In hospital bed 420A. Drugged sleepy. Vietnam
on TV. My aunt dreams of helicopters
cutting into jungle. Bouquets crowd its floor,

overwhelming snipers with petal-stench. She
wakes, wishes she were popular. The stroke
in 420B gets no felt daisy in a milk-glass vase:

kimono in a coma gets roses, roses, roses.
420B, soused daily with Estée Lauder
by a gassy daughter who doesn't watch

the right soaps, annoys the scent-sensitive
420A whose husband gave her one rose,
the guilty one, every time he bought a dozen.

She retreats into the cradle of her arm
where she's not missing him. But missing.
Should the Rapture insist, her body will nod

yes. Never before has her body ever said
of course. Never again will her body ever say
completely, so she thinks as a spit bath hurts.

Gauze off behind a sterile curtain, as the news
fires up above them, a riot in static on the perched TV,
my aunt wants to know of the nurse her name, does she

crochet, do tassels? As she tells it, she invites her
to supper. The table is never set—but my aunt sends
a shawl at Christmas with a baby Jesus card that says

God Bless You, signed illegibly.

The Pocketbook Women of You-Be-Dam Holler

1.

The pocketbook women beg nothing
exotic: neither
britches nay crewcut, reading light
nay altar. They babysit their uppermost
blouse buttons, heavy-heeled and
held together with bobby pins. Simply

dressed in uncashable checks,
a pocketbook woman
chats breathy as a peephole peddler,

greets respectfully her senior furniture,
keeps my kindergarten picture
in her blue New Testament
miniature: I'm John one of three
troubled sons, 16
& suicidal. *"In Jesus' name,"*

up snaps her head from the blessing
so we quick shut our eyes just to open them,
this spasmodic amen in the sweat
of her kitchen. Soupspoons
& sinkholes, wyandotte hens.

2.

Ever-racking unweeded graves
with plastic all-occasion sprays of faded
roses, pocketbook women hum over great-aunts aslew
on Memorial Day, uncles on April Fools,
Wanda-June all July, & always a widow
from the Easter obituaries. Pocketbook women
bury pocketbook women, marry
tacklebox men, raise
boys on frog-gigging, girls
to go Krogering.

3.

Twice-seasonally permed with terminal curls,
a pocketbook woman
enters any room permanent first,

followed then by that foremost
gargoyle purse, anvil blunderbuss,
gallon-fat, perfect fit
for grocery cart babyseats, its twinbead
clasp snapped gangrene with fingerprints,

its idiot
straps attentive as rhubarb, its bull-leather
genuine with brimstone, distended with polkadot
rainbonnets & hankies hobo'd
with circus peanuts & horehound
cough drops & daddy's billfold
tendered with two dollar bucks
& a Judas coinpurse
splitting the seam of its smileyface
scattering her birthyear nickels to mix
      with the spare & long lost,
      the pocketbook chaff.

Conversation, *a fantasy*

You are even taller in the dark.   I am taller than the dark.

How did you find me here?   I heard spit collecting in your mouth.

There's money in my purse.   Never enough.

Take what you want.   All but the pulse.

I've never done anything to you.   I want to do something to you.

I'm not even pretty.   You never were.

And you want me anyway?   I always wanted you.

Do you hear the sirens?   I'll take them with me when I leave.

THE LAST CALL

Half-Right Hymn

When the stone rolls away at night
her guitar blacks out with me

She takes me up, me—the prophet
who drowned right in the wrong sea

Buckshot

Eunice, daughter. Prodigy. At three played
boogie. Did "Darktown Strutters'" on the sly

for her daddy. Nothing but church & anthem for her mother,
the minister, whose tongues or silences certified the day holy

or not. Did Bach
      like math
for white ladies. On the other side of eighty-eight
      keys, adding up
to compensation, her blues

played with eyes closed, hands ecstatic—the first black
classical pianist. Almost. Rent snagged her in Atlantic City; she hushed

drunks with Rachmaninoff. At the bar between sets she sits in a chiffon dress
drinking milk from a tall glass. She changes

her name.

Nina Simone, a local rumble. Bethlehem's duped star.
Ezekiel's wheels carouse under the mahogany of her piano while royalties

get pinched. She does not own her own songs. Her contralto is a bruise
on the air. Black is the color of her true love's hair. Vengeance is mine

sayeth the songbird. *Life* accuses her of jungle jazz, shebang & Afro
topknot—pride rasping on its edge. She is called Priestess, scary charmer, fire

breather, ghostly
      yet barking.
Witch Doctor. Pirate Jenny. Obeah. A household name
      for revolution.
Extremist. Extremely realized.

Regal. Raunchy. Silken. Singed. Her piano on Carnegie's stage heaves
like a freighter. She plays the emergency ward. She commands the scene

or condemns the scene, fucking the house over when it goes to the bar
during a ballad, during the showtune for which the show hasn't been written

yet.

Tax evader. Rioter. If she'd been there when they called her mother
Auntie she would have burnt the whole goddamned place down. She damns

Mississippi, Birmingham, Atlanta. *It is finished.* Fly to Africa. Expatriate.
Prophet: *You're all gonna die & die like flies.* Slighted Diva—her blade

switch-happy & daring.
      You Al Capone,
I'm Nina Simone. 20,000 at Randalls Island. 500 at Village Gate.
      Twice she asked them
to keep it down

while she tended her garden in the south of France. Two teenagers
scandalizing their own poolside with racket. So buckshot, scattershot,

over the hedge she fires back. Princess Noire.
      Superstar. Right now. *Right.*

Now.

Give Me a Word for All This

Give me a word for

the slip of twitch between hello
and *hello:* a nod from a man you
want to know but don't: dog sigh:

bad dart: your barstool set
on a wobble: that stumble that
catches itself from stumbling:
the deep zip of sobriety when
police eye your jaywalking
alone heartbroken fatalistic
as a strut into rush hour traffic.

It's 2:30 a.m. Give me a word for

gentle movements in a crowd
cornered by last call: back-stepped
goodbye to the man you know too
well won't ever know you well
enough: scratching on a sunken
eight: u-turning sirens: wrong
number ringing in your pocket:

the mistakes kicking us into being:
the lines broken and re-broken into this:
the giving up of ghosts: nodding *yes* to no.

Not Even Liebestraum

Dizzy nothing blue show your hell-red petticoats
to an empty room. Not words I like, not liebestraum, not flash bulbs, not when
       the houseplants are dying;
only the bell I want, the abortion of its clapper.

I watch how bodies go plural, gather each other limb by stretching limb;
how in other houses tremendous fires are banked this way & burn
with perambulating anniversary; how boys lounge on futons
       in the arrangement of gladiolas
& when I walk in on them, their arms reach into sleeves & they nevermind
       the buttons.

Domelight

Brights caught
in the curl of a blown tire. Rain
on the curve. I know where to go. Tonight
another trick
kicks back the passenger seat. At
the corner of two tiger-lily'd backroads
I am daring the moon to forbid us.

5 10 20 30 40 50 55 60 70 80 85

These blue numbers mull over us, dash over
denim under a bad-boy sky that won't tell
your wife, my father, the minutes
of this meeting, this midnight on a dotted line, my miles

119,235.007. Your last name

unknown. First name like mine perjured. Somebody
junior, I remember that much. You call me
kimosabe and *brat*
and I don't like it. You are silent and
I want you to call me names. You bitch
about your lost wallet. Your broken heart
by Shannon, some waitress or in-law or
that cunt. You wear a shirt with snaps. Seek. Scan.

Tune. Fade. Vent. Emergency. Cruise. Nipple

by wedding ring, *you let me.* Whiskey
spills in the artificial evergreen, the interior
humid with breath
and private hair. You are migrant with belly. You are
trade. You hike my shirttail. You are escapee lugging
a philosophy degree. You complicate
the seat belt. You can't get off. Or you
do. You write a phone number on my arm

and look me in the eye as if trying to catch a glimpse
of something. Tonight
while rain makes full every dimple on the hood, do I
look like my alias? You want the domelight on.

We hold each other with masturbators' hands.

After That Night in the Parking Garage

To be avoided. To be hung up on.

I am the last thing. You've given up Friday nights
since you saw me that Friday night. I know—

I've gone out every Friday night since I saw you
that Friday night. I know I'm the very last thing.

The door guy says he hasn't seen you in months.

I'm all tied up in caution ribbon.
I'm holding in your shotgun smoke.

To be paranoid about. To be skirted
like a bad neighborhood. Bad
penny. Step the long way around me.

I've been getting along normally for a while now
but I have a plan.

I'm off that medication that made me gain so much weight.
I'm going to end up some Friday night

at a party you're playing.

The door guy heard you're in a band.
But he might be confusing you with someone else.

(To be seen first—before I see you.)

In Minor Places, *a fantasy*

AM radio in a stash tin, stashed
in a glove box and buried at the prepay island of a gas station:
      every song warbles like a fume.

Behind the couch on the wrong side
of the tracks in your mother's cigarette purse:
      a lighter with your name on it.

You will see your own way from now on.
Go on. There is glory where the sun don't shine.

Sooner

Forgive my trashed hand. This writing invites you

to walk a winter tire track over to my side of the house
where you'll make an unringing telephone irrelevant. This
invites you to sneak out of a party where everyone

likes you. To get out. To chill out chill out wherever
you are—just don't stay long enough to get found out: less mutt than me
at the brie, how pretty your teeth. To sooner or later get it

    in writing   like   this

invites you to comb your hair at my mother's kitchen table—
to part yourself right here, banglessly, to fold and tear yourself along dotted line

    like a tax return

while I shield you from the open microwave with my very own
albeit pigeon-toed body. This invites you to be my faux pas.

    Run to me, run. Run the length of your chain to get at me.

With two quarters in your pocket and the wrong spare key,
you are invited. This invites you

to rot a while with me, that's all—to disintegrate,
to make yourself small enough to turn around in a cabinet,
to bring everything you can carry in a thermos cap, and

    we'll find out how they live down there.

Crooked County (At The Bluebird with You)

Belly to the back of her double bass, 7 months
pregnant & hot as hell—swat, pluck, wail

& make me jealous. I want to be that baby.

Old Slew Foot, Jr. I want to be borne of that
bass-belly into this tavern smoke & tied by her

mean strings. And you, you sit behind me: you

& your shit-eating grin & your tapping foot &
your dare whispered into my ear to write a poem

of all things before I pass out tonight drunk

& over-toked at 4 a.m. when the rest of the world
is usually chasing me out of their dirty chat rooms.

You point out the girl who gave you something

you can't get rid of. She sways shyly to a cocaine stomp.
I used to be jealous but all I worry about now is your bike

outside without a lock. On stage the baby kicks & I

cross a bridge to momma's sloping shoulder. Her
fingers sting & she sings about falling into rings of fire.

Buddy, you got to know I want you but I'd trade you

in half a shot to have that whiskey voice, *big around
the middle & broad across the rump.* Looks a lot like me.

TEETH IN THE GARDEN & OTHER EVIDENCE

Proof

When I was 5   I searched for corpses
in our neighborhood   blótter-bearded
bible salesmen   & suicides
There was always   a body in the trunk
sometimes two   both men
holding each other   dying like that

There were teeth   in our garden
scattered like seeds   & signatures
burnt up in the stove   I saw motive
even in my father   praying at bedtime
for nightblue policemen   to take me
to some other house   There were black hairs
in my sheets   & a shoulder
blooming moonlight   gentle murderer
turning from your corner   to kiss me goodnight

■

When I was 25   I searched for lovers
never keeping one   just details
braided suspenders   pallbearer's cuff
grief kiss   tiger lilies
closing at dark   while we slept
& religion itself   holding its tongue

There is more to be said   of one who
moved me   like thread on a bobbin
I left him letters   dated/signed
roses polaroids   & 45s
My unhinged   woo cursive in
his dresser drawer   proves
I was held once   like steam
holds the bevels   of heavy mirrors
like fire mindless   holds its houses

Drama

smoke tonight to unlearn the body
(the salve on your chest: a tectonic melody)

the christmas tree is put away
our yard nailed shut is angry at january

hashish goodnight you'll sleep alone
(naomi's tea with afghan & television)

you drink each cup down to the bone
(the tea leaves tell you the sky is blackening)

the apartment is not holding
it sneaks in the wind; the neighbors know you're going

(i run the vacuum like a gelding)
(set the dishes loose; wring the towel & start folding)

Trash w/ Dog

In the unlikely
event of any kind don't go to the police
in puff sleeves to complain about a phone ruffian

pushing a Bents, Dents & Orphans fetish over your
answering machine. They know your trailer number

already. The police know everything. They know
your dog's name, your t-cell count, your hours

online surfing galleries of amateurs naked on
ugly couches. They know your chat circle:

      masochistic twinks who think you're butch,
      a Latino Daddy who doesn't know Spanish,

      the senior citizen who calls himself *Le Pisseur.*

They know you
smoke 24/7. They

take notes: that your mom is a bitch with a good

sad heart like any mother in the Heights behind
the Buick dealership on Highway 35 where

you're dying. *California Heights.* Every street
a city. San Diego Lane dead-ends at two A frames,

grass is cragging Los Angeles. Car dealers
make jokes about trailer 69 with its rear view

of "The Bay"—that cruised lake where
the wrong twin got decapitated. At the intersection

of major faults, you dream

recklessly.
Zebras herd

in the frost of an octangular

mirror. In mom's room, now your sick room,
two beds make a full, its comforter loud with stripes.

Your map of the world covers the window. Side effects
include yawn, tremor, sleeplessness. Jailtime

nags as a fantasy, the glory of being so wanted so
brutally. You love dirty praise. And men in blue

know you do. And they know you miss me,
cocaine and ecstasy, and mom when she's gone

to work at night. It's okay. I'm with you, our
talks inaudible to bugs. Not long ago you were

my little brother by thirteen minutes, named
Paris on Saturday nights, faggot in drag

at the height of *out*. On stage. At the lake. It was *her*
he wanted. What to do with such a fact? That night after

the bar closed, you were tripping in after-hours heels,
in no mood for tricks. Like my murderer. He called me

Paris. He said *I enjoyed your show.* He said
he had to get something out of the trunk. The police

know every detail except one.
                    They know you—

addict and convict, AIDS biscuit, trash with poodle,

he she or it . . . you
should be dead not

me. And you will be, your body alive online

                        is dying in bed.
In the unlikely event of any kind,

give yourself up. You're so close to me
now. *Evening in Paris.* The bodiless

are plagueless. Your body online electric, it shines
like a downtown fog. The men you trick now—

with a purr and a click now, their usernames
hunted and pecked, their confessions

an epidemic of type-o's—they see your body
perfect. Sizzling. Like our mother's hands dosed

with peroxide. Like stars cut into lines. The moon
on a dragged lake. Acid. Here in a version

of California, ecstasy is imported, 30 a hit. To take
Paris into town again, on X again, to mingle attached

at the blindspot. Out and about. To riot.

To dance fantastically
slutty under blacklights

at Club Paradise. Our bodies exact in the remix.

Hospice Rattle

Teeth slip when I speak a word
I taste blood with prayer
There are no nurses to call for
living in the last chamber

Outside the walls a helicopter
plays the menace, plays the buzzard
Living in the last chamber
lost moths riot the floorboards

There is no counter to clockwise
living in the last chamber
where a gaining light downstairs
beckons moths breathing ether

Living in the last chamber
with only murmurs of physicality
the debilitating conversation
of sickness and its body

Drama II

There was something I was supposed to do.

Not shut the door to our room. Not hang
your shirts on a sad line. Not sleep.

No—it's not the watch broke just the band.

I wish you were here to remind me.
Every dandelion has been plucked from the yard,
bouquet enough to be held by a clothespin.

There was something we never did tell each other.

Evidence

I saw it: six side-buttons on each black shoe
in lower than lowest morning light

palms up derby down dead with his shirt wide
open & his mouth wider open & his eyes

widest from staring at pigeon-shat celestials,
at the cooing groin of the overpass. On the ground

level trunk line he reeked of trains whoring by
& dew. There was a body I saw it. Joyrider—

facedown under a stone, wrists tied behind
her back; flush knuckles & lurid curl,

her pulse spooled away. Bachelor—
his shirttail grieving for his belt, paisleys

humping at every corner of the living room
throw. I saw it in fisheye. There was a body:

bartender like my uncle jiggered with blood,
dead woman née housewife a prayer folded

in blood. The vanity shifted—its casters
sore, its mirror bowing over an unmade bed.

There was my mother, her right hand cut back
like a weed. I saw. Virgin husked of cardigan

& sainted by sulphur, clawing at blonde grass
in the noon-daggered hour of a ladderbacked day

when gas jets whisper the maiden names of tenement
daughters & gangsters bleed thwartwise the grain

of barroom floors. The ceiling trapped in pupillary,
murder in a ring of light. There was a body.

Nurse, *a fantasy*

I've come to worry   under his roof again.
I've come to live   with a dying man
who doesn't know bed   from bedpan. My father,

his body is mine now.

He doesn't know me from Adam.
Like we never hated each other.

Archaeology

Headfirst I find you   in the ground
with your hat off,   standing alone
With spoons I exhume   you from the ground
father of cruelty,   your pants undone

Who dare bury you,   take your good belt
(old unblinking dead   man in the ground)
The rain ate starch,   your mudheart swelled
only god this deep is   mummed by the ground

Headfirst I find you   in the ground
your collar opened,   your chin unshaved
Your fingers numb   bulbs in the ground
jut for spring,   to break the grave

Notes

"Strange Valentine": For Juanita Brunk.

"Married Women: A Sideshow": *In memoriam* Martha McRaven of Anna, Illinois (1951–1996).

"Mema's Hat" and "Mema's Funeral": *In memoriam* Louise Shotliff of Joppa, Illinois (1921–1999).

"Threading Needles, *a fantasy*": Frieda Pushnick was born in 1923 with no legs and stumps for arms. Accompanied by her mother and sister, she traveled the sideshow circuit billed as "Half-Girl" or "The Human Torso." On stage, she was known for gender-normative talents like sewing, crocheting, typing, and putting on her own makeup.

"The Radium Dial": Based on Carole Langer's documentary *Radium City* (1987). Dedicated to Langer, to Marie Rossiter, and to the persistent geiger-man Ken Ricci. In 1948, Argonne, a $65,000,000 atomic research project, opened just seventy miles from Ottawa, Illinois (home of Radium Dial/Luminous Processes factories); results were not disclosed to the thousands of former dial painters tested there. *The Lucy and Desi Comedy Hour* alluded to in section seven is titled "Lucy Hunts Uranium" (aired in 1958).

"Thalidomide": Used as a tranquilizer as well as in combination with other drugs, sixty-four million tablets containing thalidomide were sold by 1961. Eight to twelve thousand infants were deformed by this woefully undertested drug, five thousand of them surviving childhood. See *Dark Remedy: The Impact of Thalidomide and Its Revival as a Vital Medicine,* by Trent Stephens and Rock Brynner (2001).

"The Smallest Woman in the World Who Once Posed on the Lap of the Richest Man in America Considers the Bad Dreams of the Tallest Man Who Ever Lived": "The Tallest Man Who Ever Lived," Robert Wadlow (1918–1940), refused the sideshow but did make money as a sort of traveling self-exhibition, with Q & A, often sponsored by shoe stores. My grandmother "saw" him in Anna, Illinois, in 1939. Lya Graf (née Schwartz) (1913–1944) was titled "The Smallest Woman in the World," but that title really belongs to Lucia Zarate (1864–1890). Graf became famous in 1933 when she posed on J. P. Morgan's lap for a publicity photo, returning home to Germany two years later. Arrested as a "useless person," Graf was sent to Auschwitz in 1944.

"After the Accident: The Evenings & the Nights of Cole Porter": Based on the
Cole Porter documentary *You're the Top* and gossip in Gerald Clarke's
biography of Truman Capote, *Capote* (1988).

"Ugly Dares the Marriage Vow": Julia Pastrana (1834–1860) "defined" ugliness
in the nineteenth century. From a twenty-first-century perspective,
her story (the story of her body and her infant's body) defines
exploitation.

"She Talks a Mile a Minute": Years ago, "Klondike 5" or KL5 indicated to a
telephone operator the number 555, which was actually the fictional
prefix for any phone number mentioned on a television show or
in a novel or film.

"The Pocketbook Women of You-Be-Dam Holler": You-Be-Dam Holler is a
bottom in Southern Illinois, not far from the Mississippi River.

"Half-Right Hymn": For Patti Smith.

"Buckshot": Nina Simone was seventy when she died in 2003. This poem draws
on an array of poems and songs (by Nikki Giovanni, Paulette C.
White, Lauryn Hill) about Nina Simone, reviews of her albums and
concerts (Albert Goldman in *Life,* among others), and interviews and
articles about her (especially Maya Angelou's "Nina Simone: High
Priestess of Soul" in *Redbook,* November 1970); as well: Simone's
autobiography *I Put a Spell On You* (1991). Her repertoire includes
Gershwin's "I Loves You, Porgy" (her first hit in 1958 for Bethlehem
Records), Brecht and Weill's "Pirate Jenny," and "Obeah Woman"
(from *It Is Finished!,* her last album before emigrating to Africa in the
mid-1970s). Many of her own compositions served as Civil Rights
Movement anthems: "Mississippi Goddam," "Four Women," "Young,
Gifted & Black," and—cowritten with Langston Hughes—"Backlash
Blues." The poem's title refers to reports circulated in the mid-1990s
that Nina Simone in Aix-en-Provence received a suspended sentence
for firing buckshot at noisy neighbor kids.

"Not Even Liebestraum": Liszt's "Liebestraum" is the last (and most commonly
known) of his nocturnes whose general title is *Liebestraume*
("Love Dreams").

"In Minor Places, *a fantasy*": For Will Oldham.

"Crooked County (At The Bluebird with You)": For Merrie Sloane, vocalist/ bassist for the band Crooked County, and her daughter Maybelle. Italicized text is from "Old Slew Foot," a country standard by James Webb and Howard Hausey about a bear that's "never been caught, never been tree'd."

"Trash w/ Dog": *In memoriam* Michael David Miley. This poem is loosely informed by the circumstances of his murder in Southern Illinois in 1988.

"Evidence": Inspired by crime scene photos (1914–1918) discovered, compiled, and re-investigated by Luc Sante in his book *Evidence* (1992). The negatives are glass, and years of moisture have ghosted their scenes with watermarks that print as rings of light ("elliptoid rings") around every corpse.

Other Books in the Crab Orchard Series in Poetry